Ben Franklin's
WIT & WISDOM

PETER PAUPER PRESS, INC.
WHITE PLAINS • NEW YORK

Published by:
Peter Pauper Press, Inc.
202 Mamaroneck Avenue
White Plains, NY 10601
ISBN 0-88088-190-9
Printed in Hong Kong
7   6   5   4   3

Ben Franklin's
WIT & WISDOM

The wise sayings which follow come from many different numbers of Ben Franklin's *Poor Richard's Almanack*. Of course not all the sayings here are original with old Ben, for he included in *Poor Richard*, along with his own, proverbs copied or adapted from other collections — but he usually gave to them a flavor of his own. The woodcuts are adapted from the crude cuts of Joseph Crawhall.

WITH the old Almanack and the old Year, Leave thy old Vices, tho' ever so dear.

A little well-gotten will do us more good, than lordships and sceptres by Rapine and Blood.

Many a long dispute among Divines may be thus abridged, It is so: It is not so; It is so: It is not so.

Ill Customs and bad Advice are seldom forgotten.

He that riseth late, must trot all day, and shall scarce overtake his business at night.

He that speaks ill of the Mare, will buy her.

Fish and Visitors stink after three days.

How few there are who have courage enough to own their Faults, or resolution enough to mend them!

He that can compose himself, is wiser than he that composes books.

A country man between two law-yers, is like a Fish between two Cats.

After crosses and losses, men grow humbler and wiser.

The worst wheel of the cart makes the most noise.

Well done is better than well said.

There are three faithful Friends —an old Wife, an old Dog, and ready Money.

He that can travel well afoot, keeps a good horse.

Who has deceiv'd thee so oft as thy self?

A traveller should have a Hog's nose, a Deer's legs, and an Ass's back.

No better relation than a prudent and faithful Friend.

An honest Man will receive neither Money nor Praise that is not his due.

Avoid dishonest gain: no price Can recompense the pangs of vice.

There are more old Drunkards than old Doctors.

Harry Smatter, has a Mouth for every Matter.

'Tis a well spent penny that saves a groat.

Many Foxes grow grey, but few grow good.

Content makes poor Men rich; Discontent makes rich Men poor.

If your head is wax, don't walk in the Sun.

Genius without Education is like Silver in the Mine.

DEARE WYFE

You can bear your own Faults,
why not a Fault in your Wife?

Doing an Injury puts you below your Enemy; Revenging one makes you but even with him; Forgiving it sets you above him.

Great Good-nature, without Prudence, is a great Misfortune.

An infallible Remedy for *Toothache*, viz. — Wash the root of an aching Tooth, in *Elder vinegar*, and let it dry half an hour in the Sun; after which it will never ache more.

A Pair of good Ears will wring dry an hundred Tongues.

A penny saved is two pence clear. A pin a-day is a groat a-year. Save and have.

Every little makes a mickle.

Keep thy shop, and thy shop will keep thee.

Beware, beware; he'll cheat without scruple, who can without fear.

If you would have Guests merry with cheer, be so yourself, or so at least appear.

The poor Man must walk to get meat for his stomach, the rich man to get a stomach for his meat.

Avarice and Happiness never saw each other, how then should they become acquainted?

The family of Fools is ancient.

The King's cheese is half wasted in parings; but no matter, 'tis made of the People's milk.

There's many witty Men whose brains can't fill their bellies.

He that would live in peace and at ease, must not speak all he knows, nor judge all he sees.

Be slow in chusing a Friend, slower in changing.

Let all Men know thee, but no man know thee thoroughly: Men freely ford that see the shallows.

When Knaves fall out, honest men get their goods: When Priests dispute, we come at the Truth.

Experience keeps a dear school, yet Fools will learn in no other.

How many observe Christ's Birthday; How few his Precepts! O! 'tis easier to keep Holidays than Commandments.

He that drinks his Cyder alone, let him catch his Horse alone.

Who is rich? He that rejoices in his Portion.

The Devil wipes his Breech with poor Folk's Pride.

A ship under sail and a big-bellied Woman, are the handsomest two things that can be seen common.

Industry pays Debts, Despair encreases them.

They who have nothing to trouble them, will be troubled at nothing.

There is much difference between imitating a good man, and counterfeiting him.

Monkeys, warm with envious spite, their most obliging friends will bite.

Half Wits talk much but say little.

An open Foe may prove a curse; But a pretended Friend is worse.

Wealth is not his that has it, but his that enjoys it.

'Tis easy to see, hard to foresee.

In a discreet man's mouth a publick thing is private.

He that buys by the penny, maintains not only himself, but other people.

Here comes Courage! that seized the Lion absent, and ran away from the present Mouse.

Cæsar did not merit the triumphal car more than he that conquers himself.

Let thy maid-servant be faithful, strong, and homely.

Declaiming against Pride, is not always a Sign of Humility.

Those who in Quarrels interpose, Must often wipe a bloody nose.

Where yet was ever found the mother, who'd change her booby for another?

He that hath a Trade, hath an Estate.

There are no fools so troublesome as those that have wit.

Late Children, early Orphans.

Quarrels never could last long, If on one side only lay the wrong.

You will be careful, if you are wise, how you touch men's Religion, or Credit, or Eyes.

Lend money to an Enemy, and thou'lt gain him; to a Friend, and thou'lt lose him.

Strange! that a Man who has wit enough to write a Satyr, should have folly enough to publish it.

The heart of the Fool is in his mouth, but the mouth of the wise man is in his heart.

Visit your Aunt, but not every Day; and call at your Brother's, but not every night.

What you would seem to be, be really.

Prayers and Provender hinder no journey.

Half-Hospitality opens his Door and shuts up his Countenance.

Hear Reason, or she'll make you feel her.

At the working man's house Hunger looks in, but dares not *enter*.

Where there is Hunger, Law is not regarded; and where Law is not regarded, there will be Hunger.

An empty Bag cannot stand up-
right.

There's none deceived but he that
trusts.

Tricks and treachery are the prac-
tice of Fools that have not wit
enough to be honest.

Fear not Death; for the sooner
we die, the longer shall we be
immortal.

There are lazy Minds as well as
lazy Bodies.

When you speak to a man, look on
his eyes; when he speaks to thee,
look on his mouth.

Observe all men; thyself most.

Wish not so much to live long, as
to live well.

If you have time, don't wait for
Time.

Tart Words make no Friends: a spoonful of honey will catch more flies than a Gallon of Vinegar.

Sloth (like Rust) consumes faster than Labour wears: the used Key is always bright.

The Way to see by Faith is to shut the Eye of Reason.

As Pride increases, Fortune declines.

Drive thy Business, or it will drive thee.

A rich rogue is like a fat hog, who never does good till as dead as a log.

The Morning Daylight appears plainer when you put out your Candle.

The most exquisite Folly is made of Wisdom spun too fine.

Search others for their Virtues, thyself for thy Vices.

Hunger is the best Pickle.

Little Strokes fell great Oaks.

Clean your Finger, before you point at my Spots.

Life with Fools consists in Drinking; with the wise Man, living's Thinking.

Who is strong? He that can conquer his bad Habits.

To-morrow I'll reform,
    The fool does say;
To-day itself's too late —
    The *wise* did yesterday.

Dine with little, sup with less: Do better still; sleep supperless.

If you'd lose a troublesome Visitor, lend him money.

A man in a Passion rides a mad Horse.

The wise Man draws more Advantage from his Enemies, than the Fool from his Friends.

Each year one vicious habit rooted out, in time might make the worst man good throughout.

None but the well-bred Man knows how to confess a fault, or acknowledge himself in an error.

He that has not got a Wife, is not yet a compleat Man.

Industry, Perseverance, & Frugality, make Fortune yield.

Fear to do ill, and you need fear nought else.

Seven wealthy towns contend
    for Homer dead,
Thro' which the living Homer
    beg'd his bread.

Marry above thy match, thou'lt get a master.

Seek Virtue, and of that possest,
To Providence resign the rest.

Promises may get thee friends, but non-performance will turn them into enemies.

Enjoy the present hour, be mindful of the past; & neither fear nor wish the approaches of the last.

Many would live by their Wits, but break for want of Stock.

Tho' Modesty is a Virtue, Bashfulness is a Vice.

Hide not your Talents, they for Use were made: "What's a Sun-Dial in the Shade?"

If evils come not,
    Then our fears are vain;
And if they do,
    Fear but augments the pain.

Learn of the skillful: He that teaches himself, hath a fool for his master.

Death takes no Bribes.

E'er you remark another's sin, bid your own conscience look within.

Anger and Folly walk cheek by jowl; Repentance treads on both their heels.

Be not niggardly of what costs thee nothing, as courtesy, counsel, and countenance.

Man's tongue is soft,
  And bone doth lack;
Yet a stroke therewith
  May break a man's back.

O Lazy bones! Dost thou think God would have given thee arms and legs, if He had not design'd thou should'st use them?

No Gains without Pains.

The Creditors are a superstitious sect, great observers of set Days and Times.

Duty is not beneficial because it is commanded, but is commanded because it is beneficial.

Fools make feasts and Wise Men eat them.

Proclaim not all thou knowest, all thou owest, all thou hast, nor all thou can'st.

Great beauty, great strength, and great riches are really and truly of no great use; a right Heart exceeds all.

To bear other people's afflictions, every one has courage and enough to spare.

Epitaph on a Scolding Wife by her Husband: Here my poor Bridget's Corps doth lie, she is at rest, — and so am I.

He's a Fool that cannot conceal his Wisdom.

All Blood is alike ancient.

Tim was so learned, that he could name a Horse in nine Languages. So ignorant, that he bought a Cow to ride on.

A true Friend is the best Possession.

Great Spenders are bad Lenders.

Many complain of their Memory, few of their Judgment.

You may talk too much on the best of Subjects.

The same man cannot be both Friend and Flatterer.

He who multiplies Riches multiplies Cares.

> The poor have little,
>   Beggars none;
> The rich too much
>   Enough not one.

Hear no ill of a Friend, nor speak any of an Enemy.

Pay what you owe, and you'll know what is your own.

An old man in a House is a good Sign.

Those who are fear'd, are hated.

Be always ashamed to catch thyself idle.

At 20 years of age the will reigns; at 30 the wit; at 40 the judgment.

If you would keep your secret from an Enemy, tell it not to a Friend.

The Traveller that is struck by Lightning, seldom gets home to tell his Widow.

The Things which hurt, instruct.

The Eye of a Master will do more Work than his Hand.

Let thy discontents be thy secrets; — if the World knows them 'twill despise thee and increase them.

Beware of little Expenses: a small leak will sink a great Ship.

There are no ugly loves, nor handsome prisons.

He that would have a short Lent, let him borrow money to be repaid at Easter.

Eat few Suppers, and you'll need few Medicines.

If Passion drives, let Reason hold the Reins.

Money and Man
   A mutual Friendship show:
Man makes false Money,
   Money makes Man so.

To err is human, to repent divine; to persist devilish.

Here comes Glib-Tongue: who can out-flatter a Dedication; and lie, like ten Epitaphs.

In Marriage without love, there
will be Love without Marriage.

A Lie stands on one leg, Truth on two.

Grief often treads
   Upon the heels of pleasure,
Marry'd in haste,
   We oft repent at leisure;
Some by experience
   Find these words misplaced,
Marry'd at leisure,
   They repent in haste.

The Tongue offends, and the Ears get the Cuffing.

Ceremony is not Civility; nor is Civility Ceremony.

Mankind are very odd Creatures: One half censure what they practise, the other half practise what they censure; the rest always say and do as they ought.

An undutiful Daughter will prove an unmanageable Wife.

Glass, China, and Reputation, are easily crack'd, and never well mended.

He is not well bred, that cannot bear Ill-Breeding in others.

Kings and Bears often worry their keepers.

Light Purse, heavy Heart.

He's a fool that makes his Doctor his Heir.

A Brother may not be a Friend, but a Friend will always be a Brother.

Ne'er take a Wife till thou hast a house (and a fire) to put her in.

He that lieth down with Dogs, shall rise up with Fleas.

Beware of the young Doctor and the old Barber.

Plough deep while Sluggards sleep; and you shall have Corn to sell and to keep.

Love well, whip well.

Eat to live, and not live to eat.

After three days men grow weary of a wench, a guest, and weather rainy.

To lengthen thy Life, lessen thy Meals.

The proof of gold is fire; the proof of woman, gold; the proof of man, a woman.

Great talkers, little doers.

Take counsel in Wine, but resolve afterwards in Water.

He that drinks fast, pays slow.

Great famine when Wolves eat Wolves.

A full Belly is the Mother of all Evil.

Wise Men learn by others' harms; Fools by their own.

What maintains one Vice would bring up two Children.

A quiet Conscience sleeps in Thunder, but Rest and Guilt live far asunder.

He that won't be counsell'd, can't be help'd.

Wink at small faults — remember thou hast great ones.

Eat to please thyself, but dress to please others.

When man and woman die,
    as poets sung
His heart's the last part moves,
    Her last, the tongue.

Craft must be at charge for clothes, but Truth can go naked.

Write Injuries in Dust, Benefits in Marble.

Happy's the Wooing that's not long a doing.

He that takes a Wife takes Care.

Lawyers, Preachers, and Tomtit's Eggs, there are more of them hatched than come to perfection.

Poverty wants some things, Luxury many things, Avarice all things.

All things are cheap to the saving, dear to the wasteful.

If you ride a Horse, sit close and tight, if you ride a Man, sit easy and light.

Would you persuade, speak of interest, not of reason.

Serving God is doing good to Man, but praying is thought an easier Service, and therefore more generally chosen.

What is Serving God? 'Tis doing Good to Man.

Samson, for all his strong Body, had a weak Head, or he would not have laid it in a Harlot's lap.

He that waits upon Fortune, is never sure of a dinner.

Drink water, put the Money in your pocket, and leave the dry-bellyache in the punch-bowl.

Full of Courtesie, full of Craft.

Approve not of him who commends all you say.

You cannot pluck roses
    Without fear of thorns,
Nor enjoy a fair wife
    Without danger of horns.

A Slip of the Foot you may soon recover, but a slip of the Tongue you may never get over.

It is wise not to seek a Secret and honest not to reveal it.

Neither a Fortress nor a Maiden-
head will hold out long after they
begin to parley.

Field well till'd and a little Wife well will'd, are great riches.

Nothing humbler than Ambition, when it is about to climb.

The discontented Man finds no easy Chair.

Virtue and a Trade, are a Child's best Portion.

Take heed of the Vinegar of sweet Wine, and the Anger of Good-nature.

The Bell calls others to Church, but itself never minds the Sermon.

You may delay, but Time will not.

Have you somewhat to do tomorrow, do it today.

Love and Tooth-ache have many Cures, but none infallible, except Possession and Dispossession.

The good or ill hap of a good or ill Life, is the good or ill choice of a good or ill Wife.

What one relishes, nourishes.

Don't think to hunt two Hares with one Dog.

All things are easy to Industry, all things difficult to Sloth.

He that cannot obey, cannot command.

A house without woman and fire-light, is like a Body without soul or sprite.

Do good to thy friend to keep him, to thy enemy to gain him.

Teach your Child to hold his tongue, he'll learn fast enough to speak.

In Rivers and bad Governments, the lightest things swim at top.

Cut the Wings of your Hens and Hopes, lest they lead you a weary Dance after them.

Would you live with ease, do what you ought, not what you please.

The Horse thinks one thing, and he that saddles him another.

Love your Neighbor; yet don't pull down your Hedge.

When Prosperity was well mounted, she let go the Bridle and soon came tumbling out of the Saddle.

In the Affairs of this World Men are saved, not by Faith, but by the Want of it.

Friendship cannot live with Ceremony, nor without Civility.

The learned Fool writes his Nonsense in better Language than the unlearned; but still 'tis Nonsense.

Early to Bed and early to rise, makes a Man healthy, wealthy, and wise.

A good Wife lost, is God's gift lost.

He is ill clothed that is bare of Virtue.

Men and melons are hard to know.

He's the best physician that knows the worthlessness of most medicines.

Keep your Mouth wet, Feet dry.

If you would reap Praise you must sow the Seeds, gentle Words and useful Deeds.

Sudden Pow'r is apt to be insolent, sudden Liberty saucy; that behaves best which has grown gradually.

Many have quarrel'd about Religion, that never practised it.

If man could have Half his Wishes he would double his Troubles.

Success has ruin'd many a Man.

The thrifty maxim of the wary Dutch, is to save all the money they can touch.

Up, sluggard, and waste not life; in the Grave will be sleeping enough.

It is better to take many Injuries, than to give one.

Trust thyself, and another shall not betray thee.

Haste makes Waste.

To be humble to superiors is duty, to equals courtesy, to inferiors nobleness.

An old young man will be a young old man.

Sally laughs at everything you say. Why? Because she has fine teeth.

Diligence is the mother of good luck.

Do not do that which you would not have known.

God heals and the doctor takes the fee.

If thou would'st live long, live well; for Folly and Wickedness shorten life.

God works wonders now and then;
Behold! a lawyer, an honest man.

He that pays for work before it's done, has but a pennyworth for two pence.

You may be more happy than Princes, if you will be more virtuous.

Thou can'st not joke an Enemy into a Friend, but thou may'st a Friend into an Enemy.

Anger is never without a Reason, but seldom with a good One.

An ill Wound, but not an ill Name, may be healed.

A lean Award is better than a fat Judgment.

Eating sour Pickles won't kill your Appetite.

44

Drink does not drown Care, but waters it, and makes it grow faster.

Wish a Miser long life, and you wish him no good.

God, Parents, and Instructors, can never be requited.

Many Dishes, many Diseases.

The Sting of a Reproach is the Truth of it.

Light heel'd Mothers make leaden heel'd Daughters.

Three may keep a secret if two of them are dead.

He that resolves to mend hereafter, resolves not to mend now.

When the well's dry, we know the worth of water.

A good Wife & Health, is a Man's best Wealth.

Virtue & Happiness are Mother & Daughter.

He that whines for Glass without G, take away L and that's he.

A quarrelsome Man has no good Neighbours.

Many a Man would have been worse, if his Estate had been better.

Nothing brings more Pain than too much Pleasure; nothing more bondage than too much Liberty, (or Libertinism).

If you would not be forgotten, as soon as you are dead and rotten, either write things worth reading, or do things worth the writing.

Sell not virtue to purchase wealth, nor liberty to purchase power.

Don't throw stones at your neighbours', if your own Windows are glass.

The Honey is sweet, but the Bee has a Sting.

Keep your eyes wide open before Marriage, half shut afterwards.

The excellency of Hogs is — fatness; of Men — virtue.

Why does the blind man's Wife paint herself?

He that sells upon Trust, loses many friends, and always wants money.

Creditors have better memories than Debtors.

Forewarn'd, forearm'd.

Many a Man thinks he is buying Pleasure, when he is really selling himself a Slave to it.

There is no Man so bad but he secretly respects the Good.

Great Talkers should be cropp'd,
for they have no need of Ears.

Pray don't burn my House to roast your Eggs.

Fly Pleasures, and they'll follow you.

Since thou art not sure of a Minute, throw not away an Hour.

As we must account for every idle Word, so we must for every idle Silence.

Time is an herb that cures all diseases.

If you do what you should not, you must hear what you would not.

Never praise your Cyder or your Horse.

He that can have Patience can have what he will.

Now I have a Sheep and a Cow, every body bids me good-morrow.

God helps them that help themselves.

Good wives and good plantations are made by good Husbands.

Poverty, poetry, and new titles of honour, make men ridiculous.

He that scatters thorns, let him not go barefoot.

Drunkenness, that worst of Evils, makes some men Fools, some Beasts, some Devils.

Most People return small Favours, acknowledge middling ones, and repay great ones with Ingratitude.

'Tis easier to suppress the first Desire, than to satisfy all that follow it.

Don't judge of Men's Wealth or Piety, by their Sunday Appearances.

Work as if you were to live 100 years, Pray as if you were to die To-morrow.

The Golden Age never was the present Age.

The Wise and Brave dares own that he was wrong.

To whom thy secret thou dost tell, to him thy freedom thou dost sell.

For want of a Nail the Shoe is lost; for want of a Shoe the Horse is lost; for want of a Horse the Rider is lost.

'Tis more noble to forgive, and more manly to despise, than to revenge an Injury.

Meanness is the Parent of Insolence.

If you'd have a servant that you like, serve yourself.

Man, dally not with other Folks'
Women or Money.

Is there anything men take more pains about than to make themselves unhappy?

The sleeping Fox catches no poultry. Up! Up!

Write with the learned, pronounce with the vulgar.

An egg to-day is better than a hen to-morrow.

Tell a miser he's rich, and a woman she's old, you'll get no Money of one, nor Kindness of t'other.

The Proud hate Pride — in others.

He that pursues two Hares at once, does not catch one and lets t'other go.

Don't go to the Doctor with every distemper, nor to the Lawyer with every quarrel, nor to the Pot with every thirst.

The rotten Apple spoils his Companion.

I saw few die of hunger; of eating — 100,000.

Friendship increases by visiting Friends, but by visiting seldom.

If your Riches are yours, why don't you take them with you to t'other World?

Cunning proceeds from Want of Capacity.

What more valuable than Gold? Diamonds. Than Diamonds? Virtue.

'Tis great Confidence in a Friend to tell him your Faults, greater to tell him his.

Talking against Religion is unchaining a Tyger; the Beast let loose may worry his Deliverer.

A Flatterer never seems absurd: The Flatter'd always takes his word.

Great Estates may venture more; Little Boats must keep near Shore.

You may be too cunning for one, but not for all.

'Tis easier to prevent bad Habits than to break them.

Let thy Child's first lesson be obedience, and the second will be what thou wilt.

Rather go to bed supperless than run in debt for a Breakfast.

Blessed is he that expects nothing, for he shall never be disappointed.

Be at War with your Vices, at Peace with your Neighbours, and let every New-Year find you a better Man.

Old Boys have their Playthings as well as young Ones; the Difference is only in the Price.

Nothing dries sooner than a Tear.

A Change of Fortune hurts a wise man no more than a Change of the Moon.

Mine is better than Ours.

Dost thou love life? Then do not squanderTime; for that's the Stuff Life is made of.

When Knaves betray each other, one can scarce be blamed or the other pitied.

Fools need Advice most, but only wise Men are the better for it.

Silence is not always a Sign of Wisdom, but Babbling is ever a Folly.

Friends are the true Sceptres of Princes.

For Age and Want save while you may; No morning Sun lasts a whole Day.

He that hath no Ill-Fortune will be troubled with Good.

Where Sense is wanting, Everything is wanting.

He that would travel much, should eat little.

The hasty Bitch brings forth blind Puppies.

Two dry Sticks will burn a green One.

Praise little, dispraise less.

You may give a Man an office, but you cannot give him Discretion.

A Child thinks 20 Shillings and 20 Years can scarce ever be spent.

Willows are weak, but they bind the Faggot.

Little Rogues easily become great Ones.

He is a Governor that governs his Passions, and he a Servant that serves them.

Prodigality of Time produces Poverty of Mind as well as of Estate.

Nine men in ten are Suicides.

You may sometimes be much in the Wrong, in owning your being in the Right.

He that's content hath enough. He that complains has too much.

Virtue may not always make a Face handsome, but Vice will certainly make it ugly.

THE THIRTEEN VIRTUES:

1. Temperance: Eat not to dullness. Drink not to elevation.

2. Silence: Speak not but what may benefit others or yourself. Avoid trifling conversation.

3. Order: Let all your things have their places. Let each part of your business have its time.

4. Resolution: Resolve to perform what you ought. Perform without fail what you resolve.

5. Frugality: Make no expense but to do good to others or yourself, i.e., waste nothing.

6. Industry: Lose no time. Be always employed in something useful. Cut off all unnecessary actions.

7. Sincerity: Use no hurtful deceit. Think innocently and justly; if you speak, speak accordingly.

8. Justice: Wrong none by doing injuries or omitting the benefits that are your duty.

9. Moderation: Avoid extremes. Forbear resenting injuries so much as you think they deserve.

10. Cleanliness: Tolerate no uncleanliness in body, clothes, or habitation.

11. Tranquility: Be not disturbed at trifles or at accidents common or unavoidable.

12. Chastity: Rarely use venery but for health or offspring — never to dullness, weakness, or the injury of your own or another's peace or reputation.

13. Humility: Imitate Jesus and Socrates.

Let no Pleasure tempt thee, no Profit allure thee, no Ambition corrupt thee, no Example sway thee, no Persuasion move thee, to do any thing which thou knowest to be evil; so shalt thou always live jollily; for a good Conscience is a continual Christmas. Adieu.